TABLE OF CONTENTS

Canada's westernmost province, British Columbia, is divided into nine distinct regions: Vancouver Island and Victoria, Southwestern British Columbia and Vancouver, Okanagan Similkameen, Kootenay Country, British Columbia Rockies, High Country, Cariboo Chilcotin, North by Northwest, and Peace River. Rich in history, each region is unique to its people and land, a key ingredient to any favorite recipe.

D1315718

Distributed by:
Natural Color Productions
570 Ebury Place
New Westminster, B.C. U3M 6M8
Telephone: (604) 521-1579 Fax: (604) 522-0145

Printed in Korea

Published and copyright by Terrell Creative
and Natural Color Productions
02F0183

ISBN 1-895155-71-1

9 781895 155716

Vancouver Island

In 1776 the great British navigator, Captain James Cook, set out to explore the western coast of North America. With the discovery of the Isthmus of Panama, Europeans and Americans shared the hope that a northern waterway linking the Atlantic and Pacific Oceans existed. On March 30, 1778, Captain Cook stepped upon the soil of present-day British Columbia, the first known European to do so. His expedition disproved the northwest passage theory, however, the voyage was monumental. Cook's charts and descriptive accounts of the land and its peoples sparked trade and European settlement, changing forever the face of the Pacific Northwest.

In 1843 the Hudson's Bay Company established a trading post on Vancouver Island, marking there, a permanent British presence. As the settlement grew, Victoria emerged as the seat of government, becoming the provincial capital after British Columbia joined the Canadian Confederation in 1871.

Today's visitor to Vancouver Island will find a treasure trove of natural splendor and fascinating stops. Campbell River boasts some of the finest salmon fishing to be found anywhere. Mount Washington near Courtenay gives the winter visitor a skiing wonderland. The wild west coast has both rugged shoreline battered by the waves rolling in from the Pacific, and stretches of long sandy beaches. Smaller towns dot the eastern shoreline, each with its own local color. Offshore lie the Gulf Islands, a sailor's paradise. Victoria is the Queen city of the Island, still retaining its stately British charm.

VANCOUVER ISLAND
OVEN STEAMED WHOLE SNAPPER
WITH BLACK BEAN SAUCE

2	red snappers cleaned, head and tail intact	4	medium carrots, cut into julienne strips
1	Tbsp. minced peeled fresh gingerroot	6	scallions, cut into julienne strips
2	cloves garlic, minced	2	Tbsp. fermented black beans, rinsed
¼	cup sherry	2	Tbsp. water
3	Tbsp. soy sauce	2	tsp. cornstarch
½	lb. fresh shiitake mushroom caps, sliced thin		

Preheat oven to 450°

Rinse snappers and pat dry with paper towels. Cut 3 slashes about ½ inch deep on each side of fish. Add ginger, garlic, and salt to taste. Arrange fish in one layer in a 13"x 9" baking dish. Drizzle sherry and soy sauce on both sides. Sprinkle mushrooms, carrots, scallions, and black beans over fish and cover tightly with lid or foil.

Bake in center of oven for 40 minutes, or until fish flakes easily. Gently push black bean mixture off fish. Using a large spatula, transfer fish to a platter and keep warm. Transfer black bean mixture and pan juices to a saucepan. In a small bowl, combine water and cornstarch and stir into black bean mixture. Simmer sauce 1 minute, pour over fish. Serve with rice.

SESAME RICE PILAF

½	cup chopped onion	1	Tbsp. soy sauce
1	clove garlic, minced	¼	tsp. red pepper flakes
1	Tbsp. sesame oil	⅓	cup sliced green onions
1¾	cups beef broth	⅓	cup diced red pepper
1	cup uncooked rice	2	Tbsp. toasted sesame seeds

Using a 3-quart saucepan, cook onion and garlic over medium heat until onion is tender. Add broth, rice, soy sauce and red pepper; combine. Cover and cook on high 5 minutes. Reduce to medium and cook, covered, 15 minutes or until rice is tender and liquid is absorbed. Stir in green onions, red pepper and sesame seeds. Cover and let stand for 5 minutes.

SILVER-WRAPPED CHICKEN

The intense flavors come from the marinade, which caramelizes on the chicken as it is deep-fried in foil packets.

½	cup sugar	2	Tbsp. sesame oil
5	Tbsp. soy sauce	2	tsp. minced garlic
¼	cup Chinese bean sauce	1½	tsp. salt
¼	cup minced green onions	½	tsp. five-spice powder
¼	cup chopped fresh cilantro	12	chicken thighs, each cut cross-wise into 2 pieces
3	Tbsp. hoisin sauce	24	9 inch foil squares
2	Tbsp. dry sherry	•	vegetable oil for frying
4	tsp. fresh ginger, peeled and minced		

Combine first 12 ingredients in a large bowl, blend. Add chicken and coat well. Cover and refrigerate overnight.

Place 1 foil square on work surface with 1 corner pointing toward the edge. Place 1 chicken piece in center of foil. Drizzle with 1 tsp. marinade. Fold bottom corner over chicken. Fold sides in. Lift section of foil containing chicken and fold upward, leaving top corner of foil exposed. Fold top corner into flap. Repeat with remaining chicken and foil.

Pour oil in fryer or deep pot to a depth of 6 inches. Heat to 350°. Working in batches, carefully add chicken packages (oil will bubble vigorously) and fry about 8 minutes per batch. Use tongs to remove from oil. Drain on paper towels. Cut slits in foil and peel back, arrange on platter.

SEAFOOD DUMPLINGS WITH WASABI MAYONNAISE

¼	lb. scallops	2	green onions, chopped
1	Tbsp. fresh ginger, grated	12	won ton wrappers
1	Tbsp. rice vinegar		

Put scallops, ginger, vinegar and green onions in food processor or blender and process until just combined. Put about 1 tsp. of filling on each won ton wrapper. Wet hands and seal each won ton. Place in oiled steamer basket and steam about 3 minutes or until heated through.

Wasabi Mayonnaise:

1	cup mayonnaise	2	tsp. fresh lemon juice
4	tsp. soy sauce	2	tsp. wasabi paste, or to taste
1½	tsp. sugar		

In a small bowl, stir together mayonnaise, soy sauce, sugar, lemon juice and wasabi paste. Chill 1 hour.

CRISPY NOODLE CAKE
WITH SHRIMP AND SNOW PEAS

¾ lb. fresh or dried thin Asian
egg noodles

1 Tbsp. vegetable oil
2 tsp. toasted sesame oil

Marinade for Shrimp:

2 ⅛ - inch thick slices of
fresh gingerroot
1½ Tbsp. scotch
2 tsp. cornstarch
1 lb. medium shrimp, peeled,
de-veined, rinsed, pat dry
with towel
10 dried Chinese black mushrooms, soaked in 1½ cups hot
water for 20 minutes
2½ Tbsp. cornstarch

1 cup chicken broth
3 Tbsp. soy sauce
2 Tbsp. scotch
1 tsp. sugar
1 tsp. toasted sesame oil
8 Tbsp. vegetable oil
3 Tbsp. minced scallions
1½ Tbsp. minced peeled
fresh gingerroot
½ lb. snow peas, trimmed and
cut diagonally into 3 pieces

In a large pot of salted boiling water, cook noodles al dente. Drain well. Place noodles in a bowl, and toss with the oils. Spread the noodles evenly on a large oiled baking sheet, in the shape of a serving dish if you like, smoothing the top and letting them cool, uncovered.

In a small bowl pinch the gingerroot into the scotch, stir in cornstarch, shrimp and a pinch of salt. Let marinate for 20 minutes. Discard gingerroot.

Drain the mushrooms, reserving the liquid, discard the stems, and quarter the caps. Pour 1 cup liquid into a bowl. Stir in cornstarch, broth, soy sauce, scotch, sugar and sesame oil.

Preheat the broiler. Brush the top of the noodle cake lightly with 1 Tbsp. of vegetable oil and broil, close to heat, for 5 - 7 minutes or until crisp. Invert the noodle cake onto another oiled baking sheet, brush it lightly with 1 Tbsp. of the remaining vegetable oil, and broil it for 5 - 7 minutes more. Keep the noodle cake warm in a 250° oven.

In a wok, heat 4 Tbsp. vegetable oil over high heat until it just begins to smoke. With a slotted spoon add shrimp. Stir fry shrimp mixture for 1-2 minutes or until shrimp are just cooked through. Transfer the shrimp with a slotted spoon to sieve to drain. Discard oil in wok.

In wok heat 2 Tbsp. vegetable oil over high heat until it is hot but not smok- ing. Stir fry scallions and minced gingerroot for 15 seconds. Using a slotted spoon, add mushrooms and stir fry for 30 seconds. Stir in mushroom broth and simmer for 1 minute. Add the shrimp and snow peas and simmer for 1 minute or until the shrimp are heated through. Slide the noodle cake onto a platter, cut into 6 servings and pour shrimp mixture over.

VICTORIA'S SPICY MUSSELS IN WHITE WINE SAUCE

⅓ cup olive oil
½ onion, sliced thin
5 large garlic cloves, chopped
2 tsp. fennel seeds
1 tsp. dried crushed red pepper
½ tsp. salt
1 cup dry white wine
2 thick lemon slices
½ cup chopped fresh parsley
2½ lbs. fresh mussels, scrubbed and de-bearded
½ cup chopped, seeded, tomatoes

Heat oil in a heavy large pot. Add onion, garlic, fennel and crushed red pepper and salt; sauté until onion is light brown. Add wine, lemon slices and ¼ cup parsley; bring to a boil. Add mussels. Cover pot and cook until mussel shells open. Discard any mussels that do not open. Transfer mussels to a large bowl. Boil broth until reduced by 1 cup. Pour broth over mussels. Sprinkle with tomatoes and remaining parsley.

CHILLED CUCUMBER SOUP

1 large cucumber
2 cups light cream
1 cup plain yogurt
3 Tbsp. tarragon vinegar
1 clove garlic, minced
• salt & pepper to taste
¼ cup fresh mint, chopped

Peel, seed and grate cucumber. In a bowl, combine cucumber, cream, yogurt, vinegar, garlic and salt and pepper. Chill 1 hour. Stir in ½ of the fresh mint and use remainder as garnish.

NANAIMO BARS

Base:

2 oz. semi-sweet chocolate or 2 Tbsp. cocoa
2 cups graham cracker crumbs
1 cup coconut
½ cup softened butter
½ cup chopped walnuts
2 Tbsp. sugar
1 tsp. vanilla
1 egg

Filling:

¼ cup butter, softened
2 Tbsp. instant vanilla pudding or 2 Tbsp. custard powder
3 Tbsp. milk
2 cups powdered sugar

Glaze:

5 oz. semi-sweet chocolate
1 Tbsp. butter

Combine ingredients for base and press into a 9-inch square cake pan. Chill. For filling, combine butter, milk and pudding powder. Blend in powdered sugar. Spread over base and chill at least 30 minutes. Partially melt chocolate and butter. Remove from heat and stir until melted. Spread over filling layer. Chill.

Internationally famous, Nanaimo Bars date back to the nineteenth century. Miners working the coal fields of Nanaimo received this delicious treat in packages shipped from loved ones in Great Britain. Reminiscent of a distant home, legend claims this tasty sweet encouraged miners to produce more of the heat-producing fuel.

Vancouver Island

Formed by partially sunken mountain ranges, Vancouver Island is the largest of the Canadian Pacific Coast Islands. Extending 285 miles along the southwestern coast of Canada, the Island is a unique combination of forested wilderness, sandy beaches, and charming seaport villages.

Separated from the mainland by the Queen Charlotte Strait, Johnstone Strait, and the Strait of Georgia, travelers, along with their vehicles, are transported to and from Vancouver Island by ferry. Journeys aboard the ferry system are a pleasing experience, offering passengers a relaxing view of the region.

Southwestern B.C. · Vancouver

In a province which is larger than the US states of California, Oregon and Washington together, more than half of its three million people live in the region of Southwestern British Columbia. In a diverse area of mountains, waterways and farmlands, the richness of cultural diversity is seen in its people and its history.

Before European contact, the aboriginal people of the Coast Salish Nation lived well on the bounty of the area. Their lifestyle utilized the products of the marine climate - the plentiful fish and shellfish, and the huge cedar tree to construct shelter and even weave clothing from the bark. Their heritage remains evident in the passed down artistry of totem carving, which can be seen in many public areas.

Early trade began with the Hudson's Bay Company, which established Fort Langley on the banks of the Fraser

River. With the arrival of the Canadian Pacific Railroad in the 1880's, Vancouver, the largest city of the region, began its dizzying growth. In its little more than 100 years, it has expanded to nearly 2 million people in the Southwestern BC region, and people from all over the world flock to the area.

Ethnic diversity has made cuisine from Asia, Europe, Africa and Latin America common fare. Exotic ingredients are readily had not only in specialty stores but supermarkets as well.

Vancouver is the largest port on the West Coast of North America, shipping grains and raw materials to the Asia Pacific market, and receiving all kinds of manufactured goods. The computer and electronics industries are booming in the area, but tourism is a mainstay in the economy of the region.

It's a natural: in Southwestern BC, people say you could ski in the morning, golf in the afternoon and top it off with an evening cruise - or just come and take a walk along the miles of city beaches or mountain trails.

CIOPPINO

12 fresh clams	1 can plum tomatoes with juice
12 fresh mussels	2 cups dry red wine
8 Dungeness crab claws	2 stalks celery, finely chopped
½ cup olive oil	1 green pepper, finely chopped
2 onions, finely chopped	1 tsp. fennel
1 large green onion, finely chopped	1 clove garlic, mashed
2 cloves garlic, chopped	1 tsp. anchovy paste
3 cups fish stock	1 lb. fresh shrimp, shelled
2 lbs. ripe tomatoes, peeled, seeded and chopped	2 lbs. fresh firm fish fillets, cut in 2-inch chunks

Scrub the mussels and remove the beards. Soak for 30 minutes in a large bowl of cold water with 1 Tbsp. cornstarch.

Heat olive oil in a large heavy pot. Add all onions and chopped garlic. Reduce heat and simmer 5 minutes. Add fish stock, all tomatoes, wine, celery, pepper and fennel. Slowly bring to a boil. Reduce heat and simmer 30 minutes to 1 hour. Mix remaining garlic and anchovy paste, add to soup. Salt and pepper to taste. Add mussels, shrimp and fish. Cook covered 8 minutes or until shrimp are pink. Serve at once.

GRILLED SEAFOOD SALAD NICOISE

3 Tbsp. red wine vinegar	9 jumbo shrimp, shelled and cut in half lengthwise
1 Tbsp. Dijon mustard	12 large scallops
1 tsp. anchovy paste	½ lb. fresh green beans, snapped into 2-inch lengths
½ tsp. thyme	
¼ tsp. sugar	1 red bell pepper, roasted and cut into strips
⅓ cup olive oil	
1 lb. halibut steak, 1-inch thick, cut into 6 pieces	1 pt. cherry tomatoes, quartered
	1 cup drained nicoise olives
1 large yellow squash, cut into ¼-inch thick slices	• red leaf lettuce to line 6 plates

Whisk vinegar, mustard, anchovy paste, thyme, sugar. Slowly whisk in oil until dressing is emulsified.

Place two Tbsp. dressing in a small bowl. Arrange halibut and squash on a baking sheet, brush with dressing. Reserve 3 Tbsp. dressing for beans. Add shrimp and scallops to remaining dressing, toss. Let stand for 20 minutes. Quick cook the beans in boiling water for 5 minutes. Drain and run under cool water to stop cooking. Toss the beans with 3 Tbsp. dressing. Brush grilling rack lightly with oil. Grill all for the following cooking times. Remove each to warm platter after cooking time.

Halibut: 2-3 minutes each side

Shrimp: 4 minutes each side

Scallops and squash: 6 minutes each side.

Line 6 plates with lettuce. On each plate arrange 2 scallops, 3 shrimp halves, 1 piece halibut. Divide squash, beans, pepper, tomatoes and olives. Drizzle with remaining dressing.

PUMPKIN SOUP WITH HONEY AND CLOVES

2 Tbsp. butter	6 cups chicken stock or canned broth
2 large carrots, chopped	
2 stalks celery, chopped	5 whole cloves
1 large onion, chopped	½ cup whipping cream
1 2 lb. pumpkin, peeled, seeded and chopped	2 Tbsp. honey

Melt butter in Dutch oven over medium-high heat. Add carrots, celery and onion; sauté until tender, about 8 minutes. Add pumpkin, 6 cups stock and cloves. Cover and simmer until pumpkin is very tender, about 30 minutes. Discard cloves. Purée soup in batches in blender. Return to Dutch oven. Stir in cream and honey. Bring to a simmer. Salt and pepper to taste. Drizzle a little cream on top before serving.

CHINESE BARBECUED PORK WITH GARLIC SAUCE AND CURRIED NOODLES

Sauce to Barbecue Pork:

3	Tbsp. hoisin sauce	2	Tbsp. minced garlic
3	Tbsp. ketchup	1½	tsp. sugar
3	Tbsp. soy sauce	2-3	lb. boneless pork loin

For Garlic Sauce:

6	Tbsp. soy sauce	3	tsp. Asian chili oil
4	Tbsp. minced garlic	½	cup coriander leaves, washed, pat dry and torn
3	tsp. rice vinegar		
3	tsp. sugar		

Preheat oven to 350° and line a shallow pan with foil.

In a small bowl whisk together ingredients for pork. Put pork in a baking pan and coat with hoisin sauce mixture. Roast pork in center of oven 1½ hours or until meat thermometer inserted in center registers 160°. Cool pork completely in baking pan.

In a small bowl, stir together ingredients for garlic sauce. Stir until sugar is dissolved. Transfer pork to a carving board and slice. Arrange pork over noodles. Spoon garlic sauce over pork and sprinkle with coriander.

CURRIED STIR-FRIED NOODLES WITH VEGETABLES

1   bunch broccoli, cut into small flowerets
1   medium leek, white and pale green part, cut lengthwise into 2-inch long julienne strips.

1   medium red onion, sliced thin lengthwise
½   lb. dried rice-stick noodles
3   medium carrots

For Sauce:

½   cup chicken broth
1   tsp. cornstarch
4   Tbsp. soy sauce
2   Tbsp. scotch

1   Tbsp. sugar
1   tsp. salt
1   tsp. Asian sesame oil

In a small bowl, stir together sauce ingredients in order given until cornstarch is dissolved.

In a large bowl, soak noodles in boiling water to cover, 5-10 minutes, or until opaque-white and tender, and drain well in a colander.

Cut carrots on diagonal into ¼ -inch thick slices and cut slices lengthwise into thin strips. In steamer pot, steam broccoli 1 minute, add carrots and leek and steam 1 minute. Add onion and steam 1 minute. Transfer vegetables to a large bowl.

For Stir Fry:

2   tsp. vegetable oil
1½ Tbsp. minced garlic
1½ Tbsp. minced peeled fresh gingerroot

1   Tbsp. curry powder
¼   tsp. turmeric
4   scallions cut lengthwise in 2-inch long julienne strips

Heat a wok over high heat until hot and add oil. Heat oil until wisp of white smoke appears. Stir-fry garlic and gingerroot about 5 seconds. Add curry powder and turmeric and stir-fry 5 seconds. Stir sauce and add to curry mixture. Bring to a boil, stirring. Add noodles, scallions and steamed vegetables and gently stir-fry until noodles are well coated.

SWEET CORN
AND HALIBUT TAMALES

2 large fresh ears of corn, husks intact
½ cup packed fresh cilantro, trimmed
1 Tbsp. yellow cornmeal
1 tsp. sugar

½ tsp. salt
2 Tbsp. finely chopped red bell pepper
2 6-8 oz. 1-inch thick halibut fillets

Preheat oven to 375°. Lightly oil a baking sheet. Carefully remove husks from corn, reserving 4 largest. Lay corn ears on work surface and cut off kernels. Process corn kernels in food processor until coarsely chopped, do not purée. Add cilantro, cornmeal, sugar and salt and process just to combine. Season with pepper. Mix in finely chopped red bell pepper.

Arrange 2 corn husks on square of foil large enough to hold tamale. Spread ¼ of corn mixture, (roughly matching size of halibut fillets) over each husk on foil. Season halibut on both sides with salt and pepper. Place halibut on corn mixture. Top each with another ¼ of corn mixture. Pull ends of bottom husks over halibut and top with remaining husks. Tuck ends of top husks under bottom husks. Fold around tamale into small packet. Bake until halibut is just cooked through, approximately 20 minutes.

MANGO, JICAMA AND CORN SALAD

6	ears of corn	1	cup chopped red onion
6	small mangos, peeled, pitted and coarsely chopped	½	cup fresh cilantro
2	lbs. jicama, peeled and chopped	½	cup fresh lime juice

Cook corn in a pot of boiling salted water 2 minutes. Drain and cool corn. Cut off enough kernels to measure 4 cups. Place corn in a medium bowl. Add mangos, jicama, onion, cilantro and lime juice. Toss to combine. Season to taste with salt and pepper. Cover and refrigerate until cold.

SIMPLE CRAB AND AVOCADO SUSHI

Sushi Rice:

1	cup short grain Japanese rice	1½	Tbsp. sugar
2	cups water	½	tsp. salt
2½	Tbsp. rice vinegar		

Place rice in a colander and rinse under cold running water until water draining is clear. Drain rice in a colander for 1 hour. Place rice in a heavy saucepan and add 2 cups cold water, cover with a tight fitting lid. Bring to a boil and reduce heat to simmer rice for 15 minutes. Remove from heat. Lift lid and cover pot with a dish towel, return lid and let set for 15 min.

In a small saucepan over high heat, heat the vinegar, sugar and salt until sugar is dissolved.

Spread rice into a wide bottom bowl or shallow baking pan.

Pour vinegar mixture over rice and mix carefully with a wooden spoon until all liquid is absorbed and has reached room temperature. Use immediately.

1	large avocado	2	Tbsp. mayonnaise mixed with
¼	lb. cooked Dungeness crabmeat	½	tsp. wasabi
1	sheet nori (dried seaweed)	4	daikon sliced (radish)

Cut a 6"x6" piece of waxed paper and place it on small cutting board. Peel and pit avocado. Slice very thin.

Place single layer of slices on waxed paper. Top slices with crabmeat, spread mayonnaise over crabmeat. Cover all with sushi rice, about 1-inch thick. Place nori sheet over rice and press to adhere. Invert all onto board and cut into serving pieces. Top with daikon slices.

TUNA TATAKI

1	tuna steak	2	oz. soy sauce
•	cracked black pepper	½	oz. grated garlic
1	cup peanut oil	½	oz. grated ginger
1	oz. sesame oil	•	five spice powder to taste

Coat tuna with cracked black pepper, sear in a very hot iron skillet without oil. Let tuna cool before slicing. Combine remaining ingredients for sauce. Pour sauce on serving dish. Slice tuna very thin and place on sauce.

THYME-ROASTED CHICKEN BREAST WITH MOREL-MADEIRA SAUCE

1	cup boiling water	2	large garlic cloves, minced
1	oz. dried morels, rinsed and drained	1	Tbsp. minced fresh thyme or 1 tsp. dried
2	chicken breast halves with skin	1½	cups chicken broth
1	Tbsp. vegetable oil	¼	cup plus 1 Tbsp. dry madeira
¾	cup chopped onion	1	Tbsp. cornstarch

Combine boiling water and morels in a small bowl. Let stand until morels soften, about 30 minutes. Strain; reserve liquid. Chop coarsely.

Preheat oven to 400°. Sprinkle chicken with salt and pepper. Heat oil in a large nonstick skillet over medium-high heat. Add chicken to skillet; cook until golden, about 4 minutes per side. Transfer chicken to a shallow baking dish, do not clean skillet. Bake until chicken is cooked through, about 15 minutes.

Heat same skillet over medium-high heat. Add onion, garlic and thyme, and sauté until golden, about 5 minutes. Add morel soaking liquid. Boil mixture until most of liquid evaporates, about 4 minutes. Add chicken broth and ¼ cup madeira; boil until gravy is reduced to 1½ cups, about 5 minutes. Whisk 1 Tbsp. cornstarch and remaining 1 Tbsp. madeira in a small bowl. Whisk into gravy; simmer until thickened, about 30 seconds. Season with salt and pepper.

MASHED POTATOES
AND LEEKS WITH THYME

3	lbs. russet potatoes	6	Tbsp. unsalted butter
6	leeks , white and pale green parts only, chopped, washed well and drained	1	Tbsp. fresh thyme, minced
		1	cup whole milk
		½	cup heavy cream

Wash potatoes and place in a large pot, add cold water to cover by 2 inches. Bring water to a boil and simmer potatoes until tender, 30 to 45 minutes.

While potatoes are cooking, in a heavy skillet, cook leeks in 4 Tbsp. butter over low heat, until soft. Stir in thyme, salt and pepper to taste.

Drain potatoes and dry on a towel. Cool potatoes just until they can be handled to peel. While potatoes are still warm, force through a ricer into a large bowl. In a small saucepan, heat milk and cream just to a boil. Stir in leeks and milk mixture into potatoes and season with salt and pepper. Spread mixture in a buttered 4 quart shallow baking dish. Chill potato mixture, covered, for 24 hours.

Preheat oven to 350°.

Dot potato mixture with remaining 2 Tbsp. butter and bake, covered with foil, in center of oven until heated through and butter is melted, about 15 minutes.

GARLICKY
PAN-ROASTED SHRIMP

1	lb. large shrimp, peeled and de-veined	1	can plum tomatoes, seeded and coarsely chopped
4	tsp. sea salt	4	Tbsp. dry white wine
½	cup olive oil	1	Tbsp. fresh Italian parsley, chopped
6	cloves garlic, chopped		
½	tsp. red pepper flakes		

Butterfly shrimp. Fill a bowl with ice water, add sea salt and shrimp. Let stand for 15 minutes. Drain and dry on cotton towel.

In a large skillet, heat olive oil, add garlic and hot pepper. Sauté until garlic softens, about 2 minutes. Add shrimp, opened flat on bottom of pan. Sauté, turning once, until they are opaque. Add tomatoes, stir to mix. Add wine and cook for additional 1 minute. Serve on bed of pasta.

RACK OF LAMB
WITH DRIED RASPBERRY AND
GREEN PEPPERCORN SAUCE

1	Tbsp. butter	10	tsp. fresh rosemary, chopped
⅓	cup shallots, finely chopped	10	tsp. fresh marjoram, chopped
1	Tbsp. tomato paste	½	tsp. green peppercorns in brine, drained and chopped
1½	cups canned beef broth		
1½	cups canned chicken broth	2	1½ lb. 8 rib racks of lamb
½	cup dried raspberries	6	tsp. fresh parsley, chopped
¼	cup ruby port	2	Tbsp. olive oil
¼	cup brandy		

Melt butter in a medium saucepan over medium heat. Add shallots; sauté 2 minutes. Mix in tomato paste. Add both broths; boil until reduced to 1¼ cups, about 30 minutes. Strain sauce into a small saucepan. Add raspberries, port, brandy, ½ tsp. rosemary and ½ tsp. marjoram; boil until reduced to 1 cup, about 15 minutes. Mix in peppercorns. Set aside. Preheat oven to 425°. Combine rosemary, marjoram and parsley and sprinkle evenly over both racks of lamb. Sprinkle with salt and pepper. Heat oil in a large skillet over high heat. Add 1 lamb rack; brown on all sides, about 5 minutes. Place lamb, meat side up, in a baking pan. Repeat with second rack. Roast until meat thermometer inserted into center registers 130°. For medium-rare, about 15 minutes. Place lamb on a carving board; let rest 10 minutes before carving.

Southwestern B.C. • Vancouver

In a province dominated by mountainous terrain, it is the Coast Mountain Range, which gives the Southwestern region its distinctive topography. The range forms the definitive northern rim, capturing the warm moist air from the Pacific and acting as a barrier for most of the cold from the north. As a result, the climate is relatively mild, with winter temperatures mainly hovering above the freezing point.

The 800 mile long Fraser River, which has looped its way through the province, empties into the Pacific Ocean at Vancouver. For a hundred miles east of Vancouver, a narrow band of rich farmland surrounds the Fraser, home to some of Canada's best production of berries, vegetables and dairy products. With the marine resources of fresh fish and shellfish close by, a person need only visit a local farm market to put together the ingredients for a fabulous feast. Residents of the region take pride in their own production of fresh vegetables, and a walk through a neighborhood in the summertime shows the loving work of the home gardener ready for picking.

With its natural beauty and easy accessibility, the outdoor lover can find all sorts of opportunities for hiking, fishing, camping, boating, or cycling. Those who enjoy winter sports have easy access to Whistler/Blackcomb, one of North America's top ski resorts, or a number of other facilities.

Okanagan • Similkameen

The Okanagan-Similkameen Region lies east of the Cascade Mountain Range, a four to five hour drive from Vancouver. In the lee of the mountains, the climate changes to a semi-arid one, with cold winters and dry, sunny summers. It is ideally suited to fruit growing, and the tree-fruit industry has been prolific in the last century. The finest apples, apricots, peaches, pears, other fruits are shipped all over the world from this region. Father Charles Pandosy is credited with planting the area's first apple orchard at his Okanagan Mission near Kelowna in the 1860's. Orchards spread rapidly up and down the Okanagan Valley.

Okanagan Lake, which stretches over 80 miles north to south, gives its name to the region. Kalamalka Lake, Skaha Lake, Osoyoos Lake are a few of the many smaller lakes which dot the region and give it its appeal to the water and sun lover. A relative of the Loch Ness monster, the "Ogopogo," is the unofficial mascot of the Okanagan. The cities of Vernon, Kelowna, and Penticton are centers for other industry, higher education and arts, as well as providing the visitor welcome amenities.

The Similkameen River, which runs roughly parallel to the US border, provided the gateway through the mountains into the Okanagan. Along the River one can find mining towns such as Princeton, or historic Hedley. Keremeos, at the mid point between the Similkameen and Okanagan, is the mecca of the home canner. Fruit stands line the highway, and case after case of tomatoes and tree fruits are snatched up by people from all over.

B.C. PORTOBELLO MUSHROOM BURGER

8	portobello mushroom caps	2	cloves garlic, sliced
2	bell peppers, red, yellow, purple or orange (not green)	¼	cup fresh basil, chopped
1	Walla Walla or Vadalia sweet onion	¼	tsp. salt
		¼	tsp. ground pepper
¼	cup white wine vinegar	4	portions of favorite melting cheese; mozzarella, fontina or provolone
2	Tbsp. olive oil		

Slice each pepper into 6-8 strips; slice onion into 8 thick slices.

Combine vinegar, oil, garlic, basil, salt and pepper in large plastic bag. Add peppers and onion, seal and chill 30-45 minutes. Turn bag to mix marinade, add mushroom caps and chill for 30 minutes.

Remove all from marinade, set caps aside and reserve marinade. Secure onion slices with toothpicks. Grill onions and peppers until lightly charred, about 10 minutes.

Top 4 mushroom caps(stem side) with pepper and cheese. Place 4 caps on top and grill with lid closed until cheese melts.

SWEET POTATO CHIPS

2	sweet potatoes, peeled and sliced very, very thin	•	vegetable or peanut oil for frying

In a large saucepan, pour oil to 2-inch depth, heat to 360°

Fry potato slices in small batches until golden and crisp, 1-2 minutes. Remove as they brown. Drain on paper towels and sprinkle with seasoned salt.

ASPARAGUS PASTA SALAD

2	cups small pasta, bow tie, wheels, etc.	1	stalk celery, finely diced
1	lb. asparagus, cut into small pieces	1	cup green onions, sliced
		2	Tbsp. fresh basil, chopped
1	small red bell pepper, diced	2	Tbsp. cashews, pecans, or almonds, chopped
1	cup fresh mushrooms, sliced		

Cook pasta, drain and set aside. Cook asparagus to desired crispness, drain with cold water and set aside.

Dressing:

2	tsp. minced garlic	1½	Tbsp. lemon juice
2	tsp. course ground mustard	¼	tsp. Worcestershire sauce
3	anchovy fillets	1	Tbsp. white wine vinegar
½	tsp. pepper	½	cup olive oil
½	tsp. salt	¼	cup Romano or Parmesan cheese, freshly grated
1	egg yolk		

Put all ingredients in a blender and mix well. Combine salad ingredients and pour dressing over, toss well. Chill. Garnish with additional grated cheese.

CHILLED BERRY SOUP

750 ml.	Riesling wine	⅓	cup honey
1	vanilla bean	2	Tbsp. fresh lemon juice
1	bunch fresh mint	1	cup fresh raspberries
10	oz. frozen strawberries, thawed	1	cup fresh blueberries
½	cup water	1	cup fresh blackberries

Bring wine, vanilla and mint to a boil, reduce to 1½ cups. Cover and chill 1 hour. Pour through a mesh strainer, discard mint and vanilla.

Process strawberries and water in a blender until smooth; pour into wine mixture through mesh strainer to remove seeds. Stir in remaining ingredients. Chill.

OKANAGAN SALPICON

1	lb. brisket of beef	⅓	cup white wine vinegar
2	large onions, peeled and sliced	1½	tsp. salt
1	qt. canned beef broth	2	cloves garlic, crushed
4	poblano peppers or 6 long green chiles cut into ¼-inch wide strips	1	cup red onion, coarsely chopped
4	oz. chipotles adobado, puréed or can use dried powder	¾	cup cilantro, minced
		1	head romaine, separated
⅔	cup olive oil	3	medium tomatoes, wedged
½	cup fresh lime juice	2	ripe black skinned avocados, peeled and pitted
8	oz. jack cheese, cut into ¼-inch cubes	5	radishes, sliced paper thin
		•	small flour tortillas

Lay the brisket, fat side up, in a 6 quart Dutch oven. Scatter the onion slices over meat. Pour in broth and add cold water to cover the meat by 3 inches. Set over medium heat and bring to a boil. Cover, lower the heat and simmer, adding additional boiling water as necessary. Turn brisket at the halfway point, about 2 hours. Total cooking time about 4 hours. Remove from heat, uncover and let stand in broth until it is just cool enough to handle.

Pour off and strain broth, reserving 1½ cups. Trim fat from brisket and discard. Using the tines of two forks, one in each hand, in a downward pulling motion, thoroughly shred the meat. Should be almost fluffy. In a bowl, combine the beef and the broth and let stand covered at room temperature. Whisk together chipoltes, olive oil, lime juice, vinegar, salt and garlic. Drain the meat, pressing hard with back of a large spoon to extract any broth that has not been absorbed. In a large bowl toss together the beef, diced cheese, and chipotle mixture. Add the red onions, cilantro, chile strips and toss again. Line a large platter with the coarse outer leaves of the romaine. Mound the salpicon on the lettuce. Garnish with spiky yellow inner leaves of romaine, the tomatoes and avocado wedges. Scatter the radish rounds over all. Serve with warm tortillas.

BING CHERRY PUNCH

½	cup fresh lemon juice, strained	1	lb. fresh bing or dark cherries, pitted
½	cup fresh orange juice, strained	½	cup cherry heering
¼	cup fresh lime juice, strained	½	cup créme de cassis
¼	cup superfine granulated sugar	4	cups chilled seltzer or club soda
2	cups light rum		
½	cup dark rum		

In a large bowl combine lemon, orange and lime juices. Stir in sugar until dissolved. Stir in cherries, light and dark rum, cherry heering and créme de cassis. Chill for 1 hour. Transfer to punch bowl and stir in seltzer or club soda. Garnish with lime slices.

BAKED BUTTERNUT SQUASH WITH APPLES AND MAPLE SYRUP

2	medium butternut squash, peeled, quartered lengthwise, seeded, cut crosswise into ¼-inch thick slices.	2	lbs. medium tart green apples, peeled, quartered, cored, cut crosswise in ¼-inch thick slices
¾	cup dried currants	¾	cup pure maple syrup
•	freshly grated nutmeg	¼	cup butter, cut into pieces
		1½	Tbsp. fresh lemon juice

Preheat oven to 350°. Cook squash in a large pot of boiling, salted water until just tender, about 3 minutes. Drain well. Combine squash, apples and currants in a glass baking dish. Season generously with nutmeg, salt and pepper. Combine maple syrup, butter and lemon juice in a small saucepan. Whisk over low heat until butter melts. Pour over squash mixture and toss to coat. Bake until squash and apples are very tender, stirring occasionally, about 1 hour. Cool 5 minutes before serving.

OKANAGAN HARVEST PIZZA

Jalapeño Chicken:

Toppings for 2 7" Pizzas

2 boneless chicken breasts, skin removed	2 Tbsp. olive oil
1 jalapeño pepper, seeded	¼ cup fresh cilantro, chopped
½ cup sliced porchini mushrooms	1 cup sliced fresh mozzarella cheese
1 small red bell pepper, cut into ¼ - inch rings	½ cup fontina cheese
	¼ cup green onions

Heat 1 Tbsp. olive oil in sauté pan, add pepper rings. Sauté lightly and remove. Add chicken, jalapeño and mushrooms, sauté until chicken is just pink inside. Salt and pepper to taste, add cilantro and mix well. Set aside to cool. Preheat oven and pizza stone to 500°.

Stretch dough to desired diameter. Top dough with half the following ingredients in order. Brush with oil, cheeses, chicken, pepper rings and green onions. Slide pizza onto hot pizza stone and bake for 10 minutes.

Eggplant, Tomato and Goat Cheese Pizza:

Toppings for 2 7" Pizzas

½ lb. eggplant	2 tsp. olive oil
1 large portobello mushroom	6 oz. grated mozzarella
• olive oil	2 oz. fresh goat cheese, sliced
• salt and fresh ground pepper	4 cloves garlic, chopped
2 plum tomatoes sliced thin	• dried red chile flakes
1 small leek	• fresh oregano, chopped

Cut eggplant into ¼-inch slices. Slice mushroom into strips. Sauté eggplant in a little olive oil, quickly. Salt and pepper, remove and set aside. Repeat with portobello. Clean and dry leek. Slice white portion, discard the top. Slice tomato.

Preheat oven and pizza stone to 500°. Work dough as directed in recipe. Brush with 1 tsp. olive oil and sprinkle with chile flakes. Top dough with half of the following, in order. Cheeses, eggplant, mushrooms, leeks, garlic and tomato. Top with oregano. Slide pizza onto hot stone and bake for 10 minutes.

Pizza Dough:

4 7" Pizzas

3 cups all-purpose flour	¾ cup cool water
1 tsp. salt	1 pkg. dry yeast
2 Tbsp. olive oil	¼ warm water

Place flour in food processor, add salt and blend a few seconds. Combine olive oil and ¾ cup cool water, mix well.

Dissolve yeast in ¼ cup warm water, let stand 10 minutes.

Start motor and slowly add oil/water mixture. Then add dissolved yeast. Process until dough forms into a ball. Knead on lightly floured surface until smooth. Place in a buttered bowl and let rest for 30 minutes.

Divide dough into 4 equal parts. Roll into a ball. Place all on a cookie sheet, cover with towel and refrigerate. Let dough sit at room temperature 1 hour before baking.

On a lightly floured board, flatten each ball into a 6-inch circle, making an outer edge. Turn the dough over and repeat. Lift the dough and gently stretch the edges to desired diameter.

Place dough on a baking sheet, preferably without edges, to make transfer to heated pizza stone easy.

WARM MOZZARELLA AND TOMATO SALAD

⅔ cup olive oil	½ cup kalamata olives, pitted and minced
⅓ cup red wine vinegar	¾ lb. fresh mozzarella cheese, cut into 12 slices
2 shallots, minced	
1 clove garlic, minced	½ cup lightly packed basil leaves, sliced fine
• salt and freshly ground pepper	
4 large tomatoes	

To make vinaigrette, measure half the oil, vinegar, shallots and garlic into two small bowls. Whisk to blend and season with salt and pepper. Core tomatoes. Slice off tops and bottoms and dice; mix into one bowl. Mix the minced olives into the other bowl. Cut each tomato into 3 slices; place on platter and spoon the tomato vinaigrette over slices. Place cheese slices on another platter and spoon the olive vinaigrette over cheese slices. Sprinkle tomato and cheese slices with basil. Cover all and marinate for 1 hour. Heat broiler. On baking sheet, make four stacks of tomato and cheese slices, beginning with tomato and ending with cheese. Place under broiler; broil just until cheese begins to melt. Remove to individual plates with spatula and garnish with additional basil.

SUNNY OKANAGAN APRICOT CHICKEN

4 lbs. of chicken pieces	2 Tbsp. honey
1½ cups apricot jam	¼ tsp. ground ginger
½ cup chili sauce	¼ tsp. salt
⅓ cup dry white wine	1 cup dried apricots
2 Tbsp. soy sauce	

Place chicken in a large baking pan. In a saucepan, combine all ingredients but the apricots. Heat until well blended. Baste the chicken with the sauce and pour remaining sauce overall. Bake in a 375° oven for 1 hour. Add dried apricots, bake an additional ½ hour.

Okanagan • Similkameen

Since the 1920's, vineyards and wineries have spread throughout the Okanagan-Similkameen region. Award winning wines are produced from the many Estate wineries, the most active region of the province in the production of wines. A driving tour of wineries draws thousands of visitors to the region each year.

The Okanagan also draws visitors as a favorite vacation spot each year. Water sports abound, golf courses are readily accessible, and plentiful sunshine and warmth greet the summer visitor. In winter, ski resorts draw not only the downhill and snowboard enthusiasts, but also the cross-country enthusiast and ice fishers. It is a land for all season enjoyment.

Kootenay Country

In the stretch of country between the dry Okanagan and the Canadian Rockies lies the region known as Kootenay Country. Mountain ranges such as the Columbias and the Monashees have wrinkled the countryside into a series of long, picturesque lakes with grand mountains standing guard between.

Small towns with big stories dot the region, towns like Kaslo or Nelson, or Trail. Mining, logging, and farming are main industries, and of course, tourism, which draws people to the breathtaking scenery, the friendly people, and some surprising culinary delights from Russian, Eastern European, and Italian immigrants.

CREAMED PHEASANT

1	pheasant, cut up	½	tsp. salt
1	can cream of mushroom soup	½	cup onion, chopped
½	cup apple cider	2	cloves garlic, minced
1½	Tbsp. Worcestershire sauce	½	lb. mushrooms, sliced

Heat oven to 350°.

Place pheasant pieces in a baking pan. Blend all other ingredients and pour over pheasant. Bake 1½ to 2 hours or until meat is tender. Baste with sauce during baking.

GROUSE IN A WHITE SAUCE

2-3 breasts of grouse
½ cup flour
• salt

• pepper
¼ cup margarine

Sauce:

¼ cup margarine
¼ cup flour

1 cup milk
• salt and pepper to taste

Preheat oven to 350°. Melt margarine in an oven proof dish.

Mix flour, salt and pepper on a piece of wax paper. Coat breast pieces with mixture and place in prepared dish. Bake in oven until slightly browned, about 45 minutes. Cover.

Prepare white sauce. Melt margarine in a saucepan over low heat and quickly stir in flour. As soon as the margarine is melted, pour in milk, stirring constantly. Add salt and pepper to taste. Pour over baked grouse and bake for another 15 minutes.

GRAND FORKS BORSCHT

6 Tbsp. butter
3 large onions, chopped finely
1 medium beet, peeled and grated

1 carrot, grated
2 stalks celery, chopped
1 green pepper, chopped

In a large skillet, melt butter and sauté vegetables. Simmer for 5 minutes.

1 28 oz. can tomatoes
¼ head cabbage, finely chopped

1 bay leaf

Add to vegetables and simmer for 20 minutes.

5 potatoes, diced
2 carrots, diced
1 28 oz. can tomatoes

5 cups beef broth
5 cups water

Bring water and broth to a boil and add potatoes, carrots and tomatoes. Add sautéed vegetables and remaining cabbage. Salt and pepper to taste. Simmer 15-20 minutes. Garnish with a dollop of sour cream.

PEROGIES
"VARENYKY-PYROHY"

4	cups flour	¾	cup warm water (to start)
2	eggs	1	large onion, thinly sliced in
½	cup sour cream		rings, cut in half
¼	tsp. salt	½	cup butter

Mix eggs, sour cream and salt; add flour. Gradually add warm water until stiff dough is formed. Knead on floured surface. Divide dough into thirds. Roll to ⅛-inch thickness. Cut into 3-inch circles (Approx. 50). Place about 1 tsp. filling on half of each circle. Fold dough over the filling, creating a half circle, seal edge with fork.

In a large pot of boiling, salted water, drop perogies 10-12 at a time. Cook until they rise to surface. Drain on paper towels.

Melt butter in a sauté pan, fry perogies with onions and peppers or favorite accompaniment.

Fillings for Perogies: each filling recipe is enough for entire batch of perogies, reduce if variety of fillings are used.

Potato Filling:

5	potatoes, cooked and mashed	1	Tbsp. butter
½	tsp. salt		

Sauerkraut Filling:

1	large can or bulk package sauerkraut	1	large onion, chopped
		1	Tbsp. butter

Rinse, drain and squeeze all liquid from sauerkraut. Sauté onion in butter until tender; add sauerkraut, salt and pepper to taste.

Cottage Cheese Filling:

1½	cups cottage cheese, drained	2	Tbsp. sugar
2	egg whites, slightly beaten	¼	tsp. salt

Combine all ingredients until well blended

Traditional Christmas Perogie Filling:

1	lb. dried prunes	¼	cup sugar

Cover with water. Bring to a boil and soften prunes. Drain well. Cut in half and pit. Place half in perogie shell, fold and seal.

SWISSED VENISON STEAK

2-3 Tbsp. butter or margarine	1 stalk celery, cut up
1½ lbs. venison steak	1 clove garlic, minced
¼ cup flour	1 cup tomato sauce
• salt and pepper	• a few drops of hot sauce
3 onions, cut up	

Trim fat from steak and cut into serving size pieces. Melt butter or margarine in an oven proof skillet. Mix flour, salt and pepper on a piece of wax paper and coat steak pieces with mixture. Brown meat. Add remaining ingredients and bake at 325° for 2 hours or until tender.

Marinade for Venison:

1 cup apple juice or white wine	2-3 cloves garlic, minced
½ cup vinegar	• fresh ground pepper
⅓ cup vegetable oil	

Combine all ingredients and use to marinate pot roast or chuck steaks. Marinate for a few hours and cook venison the same as beef cuts.

KOOTENAY MOOSE POT ROAST

4 lb. moose steaks; ½ lb. each	½ cup red wine vinegar
• salt, pepper & paprika	1 small can tomato paste mixed with equal amount of water
¼ cup butter	1 Tbsp. pickling spices; tied in cloth bag
¼ cup vegetable oil	
4 large onions, sliced	3 bay leaves
2 cloves garlic, minced	

Place steaks in cold water overnight. Pat dry, and dust with salt, pepper and paprika. In a skillet quickly brown steaks in oil and butter. Remove meat and set aside. Add onion and garlic to skillet and sauté until soft. Add remaining ingredients and stir. Place meat in a Dutch oven. Pour onion mixture over meat. Cover and bake in a 350° oven for 2 hours or until meat is tender. Remove spice bag and bay leaves. Thicken with flour and water roux.

Five large lakes - the Kootenay, Arrow, Slocan, Duncan, and Koocanusa - dominate a significant portion of the region's rugged terrain. Amid the snowcapped mountains, natural hot springs fill rock-lined pools, a welcome treat after exploring the region's glaciers.

British Columbia Rockies

Lake O' Hara
Yoho National Park

Few sights in the world are as awe-inspiring as the Canadian Rockies, their jagged peaks thrusting skyward in youthful confidence and grandeur. Their lure has drawn visitors to the Southeast corner of British Columbia for over a century to marvel at the vast glaciers, the crystal lakes and the roaring rivers. One can stand dwarfed at the base of an 11,000-foot peak and feel the wonder of nature in the clear cool air, the scent of pine, and the call of a whiskeyjack flying overhead. Native wildlife thrives in this rugged country, from the lowly marmot to the mighty grizzly, elk, and bighorn sheep. About half the population of BC's elk live in the region as well as 60% of the provinces bird species.

The Rocky Mountain Trench, a broad valley which sweeps between the Rocky Mountains and the Purcell Mountains in this region, is steeped in history in places such as Fort Steele, where sternwheelers loaded lead, zinc and silver to smelters south of the US border via the Kootenay River. A gold rush on Wild Horse creek in 1863 brought prospectors to the area, and in 1898, the Canadian Pacific Railway came through the Crowsnest Pass, which is the more southerly of the two main passes through the Rockies. Where the rails came, small towns popped up, and other settlements became ghost towns, where visitors can still explore today.

The northern part of this region is home to two national parks - Yoho and Kootenay, now World Heritage sites - as well as several provincial parks. Here is where the visitor winds through peaks ranging about 10,000 feet. In the Bugaboos, skiers travel to the slopes by means of helicopter. The BC Rockies are a sight not soon forgotten.

ROASTED PORK LOIN WITH WHISKEY SAUCE

1   3 to 5 lb. pork loin with ribs intact
¼   cup olive oil
¼   cup fresh rosemary, chopped

•   fresh ground pepper
½   cup beef broth
½   cup bourbon or whiskey

Brush roast with olive oil, rub with rosemary and fresh ground pepper. Place fat side up on a rack in an uncovered roasting pan. Roast at 375° to internal temperature of 180°, check after one hour.

Remove roast to warm platter and pour off fat. Add broth to roasting pan and bring to a boil, scrapping bottom of pan. Add whiskey and simmer until slightly thickened. Slice roast into chops and drizzle with sauce.

GRILLED SQUASH

6   yellow squash
3   plum tomatoes
2   Tbsp. chopped fresh basil
1   tsp. salt

1   tsp. fresh ground pepper
½   cup olive oil
4   garlic cloves, crushed

Beginning one inch from stem, slice squash lengthwise into ¼-inch slices. Cut tomatoes into ¼-inch slices. Combine basil, salt, pepper, olive oil and garlic; blend well. Add tomatoes and squash; toss to coat. Marinate for 1 hour.

Place a tomato slice between each squash slice and secure with a wood skewer. Grill over medium-high heat for 6 minutes on each side.

CRUSTY POTATO GALLETTE

2   Tbsp. unsalted butter, melted
2   Tbsp. vegetable oil
¼   tsp. crumbled rosemary

1   lb. baking potatoes, scrubbed but not peeled

In a small bowl combine butter and oil. In a food processor or hand held slicing device, slice potatoes very thin, transparent. Brush the bottom of a 9-inch cast iron skillet with some of the butter-oil mixture and cover it with a layer of the potato slices, overlapping them. Brush the potatoes with some of the remaining butter mixture, sprinkle with some of the rosemary, salt and pepper. Layer the remaining potatoes with the remaining butter mixture and the rosemary in the same procedure. Heat the skillet over medium-high heat until it begins to sizzle, transfer to the center of a preheated 450° oven. Bake for 25 minutes or until golden brown and potatoes are tender. Cut into wedges and serve.

FRESH TROUT PARMESAN

½ cup Chablis
½ tsp. dried thyme
½ tsp. crushed red pepper
3 cloves garlic, crushed
4 trout fillets
¼ cup grated fresh Parmesan
or Romano cheese

¼ cup all purpose flour
¼ tsp. salt
¼ tsp. pepper
¼ cup olive oil
• tomato sauce
• lemon wedges

Combine wine, thyme, red pepper and garlic. Place fillets in a large, sealing plastic bag, pour in marinade. Refrigerate for 30 minutes, turning occasionally.

Combine flour, cheese, salt and pepper. Remove fillets from marinade, discard marinade. Add fillets to flour mixture, seal bag, shake to coat. Heat oil in a skillet over medium heat. Sauté fish 6 minutes on each side. Serve over tomato sauce. Garnish with lemon wedges if desired.

GNOCCHI ALLA ROMANA

3 cups whole milk
1½ tsp. salt
• pinch of ground nutmeg
• freshly ground pepper
¾ cup semolina

2 eggs
1 cup freshly grated Parmesan cheese
4 Tbsp. butter, melted

Butter a large baking sheet and set aside. In a heavy 2-3 quart saucepan, bring the milk, salt, nutmeg and a few grindings of pepper to a boil over moderate heat. Add the semolina gradually, so milk does not stop boiling, stirring constantly with a wooden spoon. Continue cooking until thick (the wooden spoon will be able to stand up in middle of the pan). Remove from heat.

Beat eggs lightly, add ¾ cup Parmesan cheese. Stir into semolina, blend well. Spoon onto a buttered baking sheet, smoothing to a thickness of ¼ -inch. Refrigerate for 1½ hours.

Preheat oven to 400°. Butter an 8-inch shallow baking/serving dish. With a small biscuit cutter, cut semolina into small circles. Transfer each to a baking dish or 4 small baking dishes drizzled with melted butter, and sprinkle tops with remaining Parmesan cheese. Bake on middle shelf for 15 minutes until crisp, put under hot broiler for 30 seconds. Serve immediately.

STUFFED ARTICHOKES

4 artichokes
¼ cup Italian bread crumbs
⅓ cup Parmesan cheese
6 small garlic cloves, minced (reserve 2 whole)

4 large sprigs Italian parsley, chopped
½ cup extra virgin olive oil
• salt & pepper to taste
½ lemon

Cut stems off each artichoke. Pull off tough outer leaves, about 2 rows and discard. Cut about a quarter off the top of each artichoke, so you have a nice clean top. With a grapefruit spoon remove choke found in middle of artichoke. Rinse with cold water and rub all over with lemon half. Place upside down on towel to drain.

Combine the minced garlic, bread crumbs, grated cheese, parsley, salt, pepper and oil. Press a little of this mixture among the leaves of each artichoke. Season with salt and freshly ground pepper. Sprinkle each with a generous spoonful of olive oil. Place in a pan standing to fit very snug or tie a string around each. Add about an inch of water, and a spoonful of oil to water, the two whole garlic cloves, bring to a boil over medium-high heat. Cover pan, reduce heat to medium-low. Cook for about 45 minutes or until outer leaves pull off easily. Add water during cooking if necessary. Transfer to a hot serving platter and spoon a small portion of the liquid over each artichoke and serve.

Towering 11,870 feet above the Canadian wilderness, Mount Assiniboine forms part of the Continental Divide. A spectacular place for hiking, native wild flowers and white rhododendrons blanket alpine meadows that open to lakes and wooded areas of spruce, alpine fur, and lodgepole pine.

High Country

High Country means diversity. A few hours travel in one direction would find a person in dry, rolling grasslands. Heading the other way, one could explore the glaciers in Glacier National park. A few hours to the north, and one comes upon the overwhelming presence of Mt. Robson, the highest peak in the BC Rockies.

The southernmost areas take in the Thompson River Valley, and the arid Nicola basin. This is the region of the rancher, the trout fisher, and the big sky lover. Cross-country skiers marvel at the miles and miles of open country and their close proximity to Vancouver. Kamloops is the hub of the region, in fact, of the province, because most of the major transportation routes by road and rail pass through there.

Northeast of Kamloops is the Shuswap, where the evergreen forests surround miles of lakeshore on Shuswap Lake and Adams Lake and boating enthusiasts can explore the long narrow lakes for days on end. Further east is Revelstoke, where the Monashee and the Selkirk Mountains meet, the site of two National Parks.

Instead of heading east from Kamloops, one can set sights on Jasper National Park in Alberta and travel by way of the North Thompson River valley. Towns begin to get smaller and sparser. Wells Gray Provincial Park is a vast wilderness, where the visitor can experience the rugged and wild nature of this mountainous region. As one continues into Jasper, the road curves through the Yellowhead Pass, in the northernmost part of the Rocky Mountains. Here stands Mt. Terry Fox, named for a Canadian hero. In 1980, his dream of running a marathon each day on his one good leg to raise money for cancer research captured the heart of the nation.

PLANKED TROUT

Baking fish on wooden planks goes back to the North American Native Peoples. Originally, fish were tied to the planks and set upright near hot coals until cooked.

1	hickory or cedar plank (check with seafood market)	•	salt & freshly ground pepper
2	trout about 2 lbs. each	•	juice of 2 lemons
		3	Tbsp. unsalted butter, melted

Soak plank in water for 1 hour. Brush both sides of plank with vegetable oil. Season trout with salt and pepper and lemon juice. Place trout on plank and brush with melted butter. Bake on grill over medium heat or coals for about 30 minutes or until flesh flakes easily. To bake in oven; place plank on a baking sheet and bake in a 350° oven approximately for the same cooking time as grill.

WILD RICE WITH PORCINI MUSHROOMS

1½	cups chicken broth	¾	cup finely chopped onion
¾	oz. dried porcini mushrooms, rinsed under cold water	½	cup finely chopped carrot
1¼	cups wild rice, rinsed	2	garlic cloves, minced
1	tsp. salt	¾	tsp. dried marjoram
1	bay leaf	½	tsp. dried thyme
3	Tbsp. butter	9	medium button mushrooms, sliced

Bring broth to a boil in a small saucepan. Remove from heat; add porcini mushrooms and let stand until soft, about 30 minutes. Drain, reserving soaking liquid. Finely chop porcini. Bring medium saucepan of water to a boil. Add rice, salt and bay leaves. Reduce heat to medium and simmer until rice is almost tender, about 45 minutes. Drain; discard bay leaves.

Melt butter in a large nonstick skillet over medium heat. Add onion, carrot, garlic, marjoram, thyme and porcini and sauté 5 minutes. Add button mushrooms; sauté until tender about 5 minutes. Add rice and reserved porcini soaking liquid, discard any sediment in bottom. Simmer until almost all liquid is absorbed but mixture is still moist, about 10 minutes. Season with salt and fresh ground pepper.

MEDALLIONS OF VENISON WITH CRANBERRIES IN PORT WINE SAUCE

1   cup chicken stock or canned broth
1   cup beef stock or canned broth
½   cup ruby port

⅓   cup whole cranberry sauce
3   Tbsp. butter
8   3 oz. venison medallions ½ to ¾ -inch thick

Combine chicken and beef stock in saucepan. Boil to reduce to 1 cup, about 15 minutes. Add port and continue to boil until reduced to ¾ cup. Stir in cranberry sauce and simmer until slightly thickened. Add 1 Tbsp. butter. Salt and pepper to taste.

Season venison with fresh ground pepper. Melt remaining butter in a large skillet over high heat. Sauté medallions about 2 minutes per side for medium-rare. Divide sauce on 4 plates and top with medallions.

HIGH COUNTRY PAELLA

2 large red bell peppers, seeded
¼ cup olive oil
1 3½ lb. chicken, cut into 8 pieces
   or rabbit to equal 3½ lbs.
1½ lb. breakfast pork sausage links,
   cut into 1-inch pieces
1 lb. mushrooms, thinly sliced
3 lbs. tomatoes, about 7 cups,
   chopped
2 Tbsp. garlic, minced
½ cup almonds, finely ground

1 lb. green beans, trimmed, cut
   into 1-inch lengths
1½ Tbsp. chopped fresh rosemary
1½ Tbsp. chopped fresh sage
2 tsp. salt
2 tsp. ground black pepper
½ tsp. saffron threads, crushed
¼ tsp. dried crushed red pepper
2 cups arborio rice
6 cups hot chicken broth
• lemon wedges

Cut 1 bell pepper lengthwise into thin strips, chop second pepper; reserve. Heat oil in a heavy 14 inch skillet or paella pan over medium heat. Add bell pepper strips; sauté until softened, about 6 minutes. Remove and set aside. Season chicken with salt and pepper. Add to skillet and cook until brown on all sides. Transfer to plate. Add sausage to skillet; sauté until golden, about 5 minutes. Using a slotted spoon, remove to plate with chicken.

Pour off all but 6 Tbsp. of drippings from skillet. Add mushrooms to skillet; sauté over medium-high heat for 5 minutes. Stir in tomatoes, garlic, and chopped bell pepper and bring to a boil. Reduce heat and simmer until almost all of the liquid evaporates, about 30 minutes.

Add green beans and next 7 ingredients to skillet. Stir in rice, chicken, sausage and 6 cups hot broth; bring to a boil. Reduce to medium heat; simmer uncovered until chicken is cooked, adding more broth if mixture seems dry, about 30 minutes. Let stand 5 minutes. Top with pepper strips garnish with lemon wedges.

SUMMER VEGETABLE RAGOUT

3 cloves garlic, minced
3 Tbsp. olive oil
12 scallions, white and pale green
   parts only, cut crosswise into
   1½-inch long pieces
½ lb. baby yellow squash, halved
   lengthwise

½ lb. zucchini, halved lengthwise
1½ cups fresh corn, cut from ears
1 cup chicken broth
3 cups small cherry tomatoes,
   halved
2 tsps. fresh tarragon, chopped

In a heavy skillet, sauté garlic in olive oil over moderately high heat, stirring just until soft. Add scallions, zucchini, squash, corn, and salt and pepper to taste. Sauté, stirring occasionally, about 4 minutes.

Add broth and simmer, covered, until squash is tender, about 3 minutes. Add tomatoes and tarragon and simmer, covered until tomatoes are soft. Adjust salt and pepper to taste.

The bunchgrass ranges of the western section of the High Country provided cattle drovers an excellent place to winter cattle headed for the gold fields of the Cariboo. With the passage of the Land Ordinance of 1860, the region filled up with settlers interested in the cattle industry. Today, cattle ranches are a common sight throughout the Nicola Valley.

Cariboo Chilcotin

Spreading westward from the Cariboo Mountains to the Pacific Ocean, the Cariboo Chilcotin region is characterized by its varied geographical features - alpine meadows, grasslands, and desert. Some 8,000 lakes cut across the landscape, offering up prize trout and a serene environment. The region's rivers are also major spawning grounds for Pacific salmon.

The rolling, forested uplands of the Interior Plateau extend east of the Coast Mountains. With the discovery of gold in the Cariboo during the mid-nineteenth century, hopeful miners flooded the area. News of excellent grazing lands and a burgeoning population encouraged cattlemen from Oregon to drive large herds northward. Thus the beginnings of cattle ranching in the Cariboo Chilcotin.

Gang Ranch, one of the largest ranches in North America, is so large it takes a day to drive from one end to the other.

Sir Alexander MacKenzie traveled this region in 1793, ending up at the small coastal village of Bella Coola, now one of few ports between Vancouver and Prince Rupert. Today, adventurers find ample wilderness to explore, or small towns such as Williams Lake or Quesnel to welcome them as they travel to Prince George.

ROASTED PHEASANT

2	2½ to 3 lb. pheasants	2	bay leaves
•	freshly ground pepper	3	carrots, cut in large pieces
2	sprigs fresh thyme	1	onion, quartered
•	vegetable oil for brushing pheasants	6-8	small new potatoes

Sprinkle pheasants inside and out with pepper and salt. Put 1 sprig of thyme and 1 bay leaf in cavity of each and close cavity with skewers. Brush pheasants with oil and put on rack in a roasting pan, breast side down. Arrange carrots, onion and potatoes around pheasant. Roast 20 minutes, turn over and roast an additional 25 minutes or until thermometer inserted in thickest part of breast registers 160°. Let rest for 10 minutes before carving.

CARIBOO CHILI

4	cans kidney beans	½	cup parsley
3	cans diced tomatoes	3½	lbs. lean ground beef
3	green peppers, chopped	⅓	cup chili powder
4	medium onions, chopped	2	tsp. salt
2	Tbsp. oil	1½	tsp. pepper
3	cloves garlic, chopped	1½	tsp. ground cumin

In a large stock pot, sauté peppers and onions in oil, add garlic and parsley. Brown ground beef in a large skillet, drain and add to onion mixture. Stir in chili powder and mix; cook 10 minutes. Add beans and remaining ingredients, cover and simmer 1 hour. Remove cover and simmer another hour. This chili is even better the next day.

ROSEMARY RIB ROAST

½ cup chopped fresh rosemary
6 Tbsp. vegetable oil
8 large garlic cloves, chopped

2 tsp. coarse kosher salt
1 7-7½ lb. boneless beef rib roast, tied

Grind chopped rosemary, oil, garlic, and salt in processor to a chunky paste. Place beef in a roasting pan. Rub mixture all over roast. Cover; chill 1 day.

Preheat oven to 350°. Roast the beef in center rack of oven until thermometer inserted straight down from top registers 125° for rare, about 1½ hours. Let stand for 30 minutes before carving.

RED WINE HORSERADISH SAUCE

1 Tbsp. butter
1 cup chopped shallots
1 tsp. crushed black peppercorns
2 cups dry red wine

½ cup whipping cream
1 Tbsp. prepared white horseradish

Melt butter in a saucepan over medium heat. Add shallots, peppercorns, sauté until shallots are tender. Add red wine. Strain sauce and return to pan. Add whipping cream and boil until reduced to sauce consistency, about 8 minutes. Stir in horseradish. Salt and pepper to taste

CHICKEN SAUTÉ WITH FRESH CHERRY SAUCE

2   Tbsp. butter
2   boneless, skinless chicken breasts
¼   cup chopped shallots
1   tsp. dried thyme
¼   cup balsamic vinegar

2   Tbsp. water
1   cup fresh sweet cherries, halved, pitted
2   Tbsp. all- fruit cherry spread

Place each chicken breast between 2 sheets of plastic wrap and flatten with a mallet. Melt butter in a skillet over medium-high heat. Sprinkle chicken with salt and pepper, sauté until golden , about 2 minutes per side. Transfer to plate. Add shallots and thyme to skillet, reduce heat to medium-low and cook for 2-3 minutes. Add vinegar and water and bring to a simmer, scraping in any browned bits. Add cherries and fruit spread. Simmer until cherries soften and sauce thickens slightly. Return chicken to skillet, simmer until cooked through and hot, about 2 minutes

ROASTED AUTUMN VEGETABLES

1½ lbs. small red potatoes, quartered
1   lb. shallots, peeled and trimmed
5   Tbsp. olive oil
1   bay leaf

¼   tsp. dried thyme, crumbled
4   cloves garlic, crushed
2   lb. butternut squash, peeled and cut into ¾-inch pieces

Preheat oven to 375˚. In a bowl, toss together the potatoes, shallots, 4 Tbsp. of the oil, bay leaf, thyme, garlic and salt and pepper to taste. Spread the vegetables in an oiled roasting pan and roast for 30 minutes, shaking pan every 5 to 10 minutes. In a bowl, toss the squash with the remaining oil, salt and pepper to taste. Add to roasting pan and roast an additional 15 minutes or until vegetables are tender.

BOUNTY BERRY PIE

Pastry:

2½ cups all-purpose flour
1 tsp. sugar
½ tsp. salt
½ cup cold, unsalted butter

½ cup cold, solid vegetable shortening
¼ cup cold water

To Make Pastry:

Combine flour with the sugar and salt in a bowl. Cut in the butter and shortening until the texture resembles coarse crumbs. Add the water, a Tbsp. at a time, and mix gently with a fork to form a soft dough. Chill for 1 hour.

Filling:

4 cups blackberries or your favorite berries
2 cups sugar
⅔ cup flour

3 Tbsp. cornstarch
⅛ tsp. nutmeg
¼ tsp. vanilla
1½ Tbsp. unsalted butter

Preheat oven to 375°. Combine berries, sugar, flour, cornstarch, nutmeg and vanilla in a bowl.

Roll out slightly more than half of the pastry on a lightly floured board. Line a 9-inch pie pan with the pastry. Fill with the berry mixture and dot with butter.

Roll out the remaining pastry and cut into 1-inch wide strips. Form lattice top. Bake for 50 minutes.

A diversified landscape lends to a variety of sights and activities. Back road explorations wind past old homesteads, grazing animals, and shimmering lakes, offering a moment free from strife.

North by Northwest

Stretching from the Rocky Mountains to the coast, and encompassing the Queen Charlotte Islands, the region of North by Northwest sweeps Northward to the Yukon border, covering nearly one third of the province. The mainstay cities are Prince George, near the geographic center of British Columbia, and the port of Prince Rupert, where grain, lumber and resources are loaded on ships bound for Asia. The Queen Charlotte Islands, an archipelago of about 200 islands, lie isolated off the North coast, preserving the Haida nation heritage and unique subspecies of flora and fauna. The Stewart-Cassiar highway connects the southern region to the Alaska highway, and travels through 500 miles of nearly pristine wilderness.

QUAIL PIE

6	quail, dressed	¼	cup diced green onions
¼	cup butter	½	cup diced celery
5	Tbsp. flour	½	lb. diced cooked ham
½	tsp. salt	16	oz. chicken broth
⅛	tsp. pepper	¼	cup water
½	lb. fresh mushrooms	•	salt & pepper to taste

In a cast iron skillet, melt butter and sauté quail that has been coated with 3 Tbsp. flour, salt and pepper. Remove quail once it is golden brown. To skillet, add mushrooms, onions, and celery; sauté until tender. Add ham and chicken broth. Stir in 2 Tbsp. flour and water. Boil and let thicken, stirring constantly. Pour mixture into a 2 qt. baking dish with quail.

Crust:

1	cup flour	½	tsp. salt
⅔	cup shortening		

In a medium bowl, combine flour, shortening, and salt. When mixture resembles cornmeal, add a small amount of cold milk, a little at a time, until it holds together in a ball. Flatten dough on a floured board and roll out to the shape of baking dish. Flute edges and slash vents to allow steam to escape. Bake at 350° for 50 to 60 minutes.

POTLATCH SALMON

1	whole salmon	3	tsp. dry mustard
4	Tbsp. butter, softened	½-1	cup brown sugar
•	juice of one lemon	•	heavy-duty foil

Butterfly salmon; remove head, tail and fins, run knife down backbone of fish until it opens flat, do not cut through. Use a sheet of heavy-duty foil large enough to handle salmon, coat lightly with cooking spray. Place salmon skin side down on foil. Spread softened butter over flesh of salmon, lemon juice and dry mustard. Cover with brown sugar.

Place foil/fish on barbeque grill over low heat, cover. Check after 20 minutes. Salmon is cooked when flesh flakes easily.

SKEWERED FISH, SHELLFISH WITH PEPPERS

8-10 oz. scallops
8-10 oz. medium shrimp, peel leaving tail intact
8-10 oz. halibut fillets, cut into ¾-inch cubes

1 red bell pepper, cut into chunks
1 yellow bell pepper cut into chunks

Marinade:

2 Tbsp. olive oil
¼ cup tequila
• juice of 2 limes

½ tsp. ground cumin
1 tsp. chili powder
4 garlic cloves, minced

Place seafood in a large glass bowl. Combine marinade and pour over seafood. Let sit at room temperature for about 30 minutes.

Brush pepper chunks with oil. Thread all scallops crosswise on skewer(s), repeat with shrimp in same manner so they will lay flat on grill. Thread fish on a skewer and the pepper chunks on another.

Place peppers on the grill and cook until softened and lightly charred, about 5 minutes. Remove to platter. Cook scallops and fish about 4 minutes per side, remove to platter. Cook shrimp 3 minutes per side, remove to platter. Divide among servings plates. Yellow rice or spiced white rice is a nice accompaniment.

LEEK AND SALMON CHOWDER

3 cups bottled clam juice
1 12 oz. salmon fillet
1 Tbsp. butter, room temperature
1 Tbsp. all purpose flour
4 slices bacon, cut into 2-inch pieces

2 medium leeks, white part only, thinly sliced
1 large potato, peeled and cubed
2½ cups whole milk
½ cup whipping cream
2 Tbsp. chopped fresh chives

Bring clam juice to simmer in a skillet. Add salmon; cover and simmer 10 minutes. Remove salmon to a plate; reserve juice. Break salmon into small pieces

Mix butter and flour in a small bowl until well blended. Cook bacon in a large saucepan until crisp. Remove bacon pieces to paper towels. Add leeks to drippings; sauté 3 minutes. Add potato and clam juice and bring to a boil. Reduce heat; cover and simmer until potato is tender, about 10 minutes. Add milk and bring to a boil. Whisk in flour mixture. Reduce heat; simmer until soup thickens slightly, stirring frequently, about 5 minutes. Stir in cream, chives, salmon and bacon; simmer until heated through. Salt and pepper to taste.

Indeed a unique region, sky-blue glacial drifts of the Fraser River Basin stand in stark contrast to the lava plains of the Nass Basin. Further west along the border shared with Alaska, Mount Fairweather rises to an elevation of 15,300 feet, the highest point in British Columbia.

Peace River · Alaska Highway

The diversity of British Columbia is exemplified in the vast Peace River Region of the province. Farmers grow plentiful crops of grains, seeds, and grasses in the fertile land of the Peace River Valley. Farther north, muskeg dominates the landscape, and the Liard River with its tributaries form the main water system. The Omenica Mountains define the western boundary of the region.

The Alaska Highway begins in the city of Dawson Creek and stretches more than 1500 miles to Fairbanks, Alaska. An amazing construction feat, it was originally designed as a military supply route in 1942, and was completed in 8 months and 12 days through the work of some 27,000 soldiers and civilians.

At Hudson Hope one can visit the museum and view fossils and footprints of dinosaurs which roamed the region in the distant past. Just twenty minutes from there is one of the largest earth filled dams in the world — the W.A.C. Bennett Dam which holds back Williston Lake, the largest man-made lake in Canada. Generally the terrain of the area is flat in the north and east and mountainous in the south and west. The Peace River region represents 22 percent of the province's land yet only two percent of the population.

BEEF TENDERLOIN WITH PEPPERCORN SAUCE

4	6-oz. 1½-inch thick beef tenderloin steaks	6	Tbsp. brandy
•	coarsely cracked pepper	1	cup whipping cream
2	Tbsp. butter	4	tsp. drained green peppercorns in brine, coarsely chopped
1	Tbsp. olive oil	2	tsp. Dijon mustard

Season steaks with salt and a generous amount of cracked pepper. Melt butter and olive oil in a large skillet over high heat. Add steaks and cook to desired degree of doneness, about 4 minutes per side for rare. Transfer steaks to a plate, tent with foil to keep warm. Remove skillet from heat. Add brandy to skillet and ignite with a match. Return skillet to heat and bring brandy to a boil, scraping up any browned bits. Add cream and green peppercorns and boil until reduced to a sauce consistency, about 2 minutes. Whisk in mustard, correct salt to taste. Pour over steaks and serve immediately.

FRESH TROUT WITH HONEY MUSTARD SAUCE

4	fresh trout fillets	⅓	cup red wine vinegar
8	bacon slices	¼	cup honey
•	salt & pepper to taste	1	tsp. Worcestershire sauce
½	cup Dijon mustard		

Rinse fillets and pat dry with paper towels. Lay bacon slices in a very large skillet, place trout on top of bacon. Sprinkle with salt and pepper. Cover with lid and cook over medium heat for 20 minutes or until flesh flakes easily. Mix mustard, vinegar, honey and Worcestershire sauce in saucepan, heat until warm. Place fillets on serving dishes and top with honey mustard sauce.

ELK SIRLOIN STEAKS

4   elk sirloin steaks

Marinade:

¼   cup pineapple juice
½   cup salad oil
¼   cup honey

2   Tbsp. soy sauce
¼   cup chili sauce
•   salt & pepper to taste

Combine pineapple juice, oil, honey, soy sauce and chili sauce. Season steaks with salt & pepper. Pour marinade over the steaks and let stand for at least 2 hours in the refrigerator, turn steaks in the sauce to coat well. Cook steaks over hot coals.